HIDDEN PICTURES

I FOUND IT!

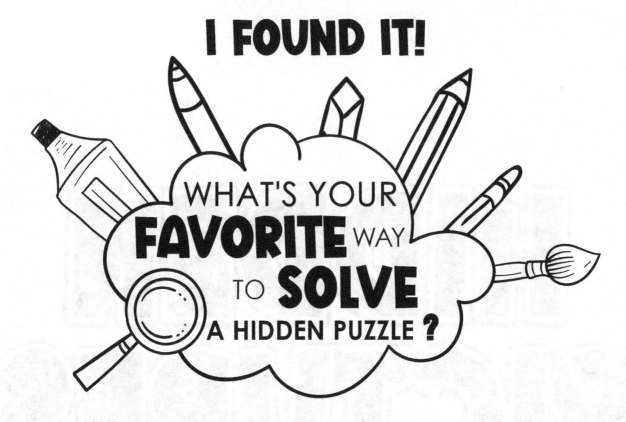

WHAT'S YOUR FAVORITE WAY TO SOLVE A HIDDEN PUZZLE?

There are TONS of different ways, including:

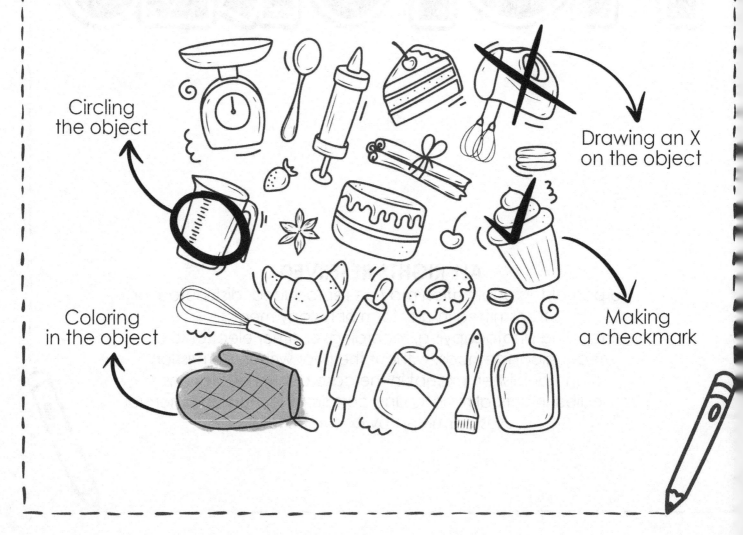

Circling the object

Drawing an X on the object

Coloring in the object

Making a checkmark

THIS BOOK BELONGS TO

....

....

....

CAN YOU FIND 8 HIDDEN OBJECTS IN THIS SCENE?

1

CAN YOU FIND 8 HIDDEN OBJECTS IN THIS SCENE? **2**

CAN YOU FIND 8 HIDDEN OBJECTS IN THIS SCENE? **3**

CAN YOU FIND 8 HIDDEN OBJECTS IN THIS SCENE? **4**

CAN YOU FIND 8 HIDDEN OBJECTS IN THIS SCENE? **5**

CAN YOU FIND 8 HIDDEN OBJECTS IN THIS SCENE? **6**

CAN YOU FIND 8 HIDDEN OBJECTS IN THIS SCENE? **7**

CAN YOU FIND 8 HIDDEN OBJECTS IN THIS SCENE? **8**

CAN YOU FIND 8 HIDDEN OBJECTS IN THIS SCENE

CAN YOU FIND 8 HIDDEN OBJECTS IN THIS SCENE?

9

CAN YOU FIND 8 HIDDEN OBJECTS IN THIS SCENE?

10

CAN YOU FIND 8 HIDDEN OBJECTS IN THIS SCENE

CAN YOU FIND 8 HIDDEN OBJECTS IN THIS SCENE?

11

CAN YOU FIND 8 HIDDEN OBJECTS IN THIS SCENE? **12**

CAN YOU FIND 3 HIDDEN OBJECTS IN THIS SCENE

CAN YOU FIND 8 HIDDEN OBJECTS IN THIS SCENE? **15**

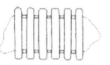

CAN YOU FIND 8 HIDDEN OBJECTS IN THIS SCENE? **16**

CAN YOU FIND 5 HIDDEN OBJECTS IN THIS SCENE?

CAN YOU FIND 8 HIDDEN OBJECTS IN THIS SCENE? **17**

CAN YOU FIND 8 HIDDEN OBJECTS IN THIS SCENE? **18**

CAN YOU FIND 8 HIDDEN OBJECTS IN THIS SCENE? **20**

20

CAN YOU FIND 8 HIDDEN OBJECTS IN THIS SCENE? **21**

CAN YOU FIND 8 HIDDEN OBJECTS IN THIS SCENE? **23**

23

CAN YOU FIND 8 HIDDEN OBJECTS IN THIS SCENE? **24**

CAN YOU FIND 8 HIDDEN OBJECTS IN THIS SCENE?

CAN YOU FIND 8 HIDDEN OBJECTS IN THIS SCENE? **25**

CAN YOU FIND 8 HIDDEN OBJECTS IN THIS SCENE? **26**

CAN YOU FIND 8 HIDDEN OBJECTS IN THIS SCENE? **28**

CAN YOU FIND 8 HIDDEN OBJECTS IN THIS SCENE? 29

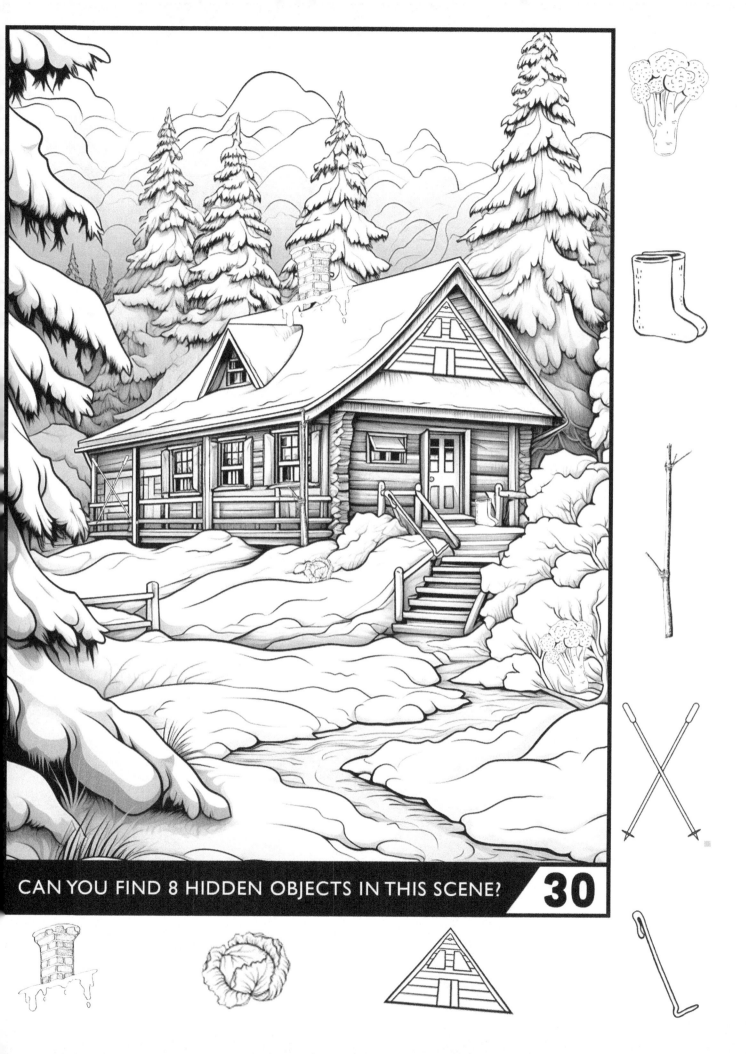

CAN YOU FIND 8 HIDDEN OBJECTS IN THIS SCENE? **30**

SOLUTIONS

LET'S CHECK IT OUT!

1

LET'S CHECK IT OUT!

3

LET'S CHECK IT OUT!

5

LET'S CHECK IT OUT!

6

LET'S CHECK IT OUT!

7

LET'S CHECK IT OUT!

8

LET'S CHECK IT OUT!

11

LET'S CHECK IT OUT!   13

LET'S CHECK IT OUT!

15

LET'S CHECK IT OUT!

18

LET'S CHECK IT OUT!

20

LET'S CHECK IT OUT!   23

LET'S CHECK IT OUT!

28

LET'S CHECK IT OUT!

29

WRITE DOWN YOUR FAVORITE ASPECTS
OF THIS BOOK:

....

....

....

....

....

....

....

....

....

....

....

....

....

....

....

....

....

....

THANK YOU FOR TRUSTING US BY PURCHASING OUR BOOKS

Your trust in us means a lot, and we truly hope that you will find joy and satisfaction in coloring our unique designs. If our book meets your expectations, we kindly ask you to leave a positive review as it motivates us to create even better books in the future. Once again, thank you for your support and we hope that our coloring book will bring a little bit of creativity and relaxation into your life.

Made in the USA
Monee, IL
24 September 2024

66299818R00057